an East End Album

Steve Lewis

The History Press

To my mother Daisy and father Charles for my East London roots.
To my wife Jan, who has stood by me throughout my life as a photographer and
brought up our children, Mark, Gary and Charlotte, single-handedly while I
was away on assignments.
And of course the seven grandchildren, Nicole, Joseph, Samuel, Amy, Arun,
Thomas and Edward.

First published 2014

The History Press
The Mill, Brimscombe Port
Stroud, Gloucestershire, GL5 2QG
www.thehistorypress.co.uk

© Steve Lewis, 2014

The right of Steve Lewis to be identified as the Author
of this work has been asserted in accordance with the
Copyright, Designs and Patents Act 1988.

British Library Cataloguing in Publication Data.
A catalogue record for this book is available from the British Library.

ISBN 978 0 7509 5658 1

Typesetting and origination by The History Press
Printed in Great Britain

Foreword

There's little doubt that London's East End is now at the cutting edge of modern-day Britain. With the financial powerhouse that is Canary Wharf, the giant Olympic development complete with high-speed rail links and shopping malls, this was the area that was at the very heart of the world for the London 2012 Olympics.

But, what was it like before the bankers and builders, architects and athletes came to town?

For acclaimed photographer Steve Lewis it was his 'turf', the home patch where he learnt his craft and honed the skills that were to take him to some of the most glamorous, and sometimes dangerous, places around the world during his lengthy career on a national newspaper.

As a photographer on a local paper in the East End, Steve was called on to cover everything from football to features and crime to glamour. For a man who has always sought to be creative with his work, and never just turn in a series of standard shots anyone else might be content with, it was to be the perfect blank canvas.

This compelling album shows a different side to today's East End and is from a time when it was a bustling but also gritty backdrop to families who had grown up there for generations, as well as the starting point for new arrivals to the country.

And if the East End was from a different time, so was the whole country. Check out some of the fashions, hairstyles and cars and it seems like a weird and wonderful new planet!

It's equally intriguing to see how, as you look through the album, Steve masters his craft and develops a style that was subsequently to propel him to work with some of the biggest names in British show business and in Hollywood too.

I was privileged to work with Steve for a number of years when I was on the showbiz beat for the *Sun*. Together we covered just about everything, from the impossible glamour of the making of a James Bond movie in a palace in an Indian lake, to the Cannes film festival to even being caught up in the middle of a riot when the French police moved in.

Steve brought the same professionalism, flair and genuine decency to everything he did. To see how it all began, in this glorious book, is fascinating.

Nick Ferrari, 2014
TV and radio presenter for LBC

Acknowledgements

Thanks must go to the people of the East End for so generously allowing me into their lives and letting me take their photographs. Thanks also to my good friends, Caroline and Geoff, for all their hard work in putting the words together for my books on London's East End.

I am indebted to the *Newham Recorder* for giving me the freedom to express myself through my camera, and to the editor of the paper, Tom Duncan, who had the foresight to predict the changes that were about to happen in the East End.

My books, *London's East End: A 1960s Album* and *London's East End: Then & Now*, are published by The History Press.

Steve Lewis can be contacted at   www.stevelewisphotography.com
He is represented by Getty Images   www.gettyimages.co.uk

Preface

My fascination with photography dates back to my eighth birthday in 1952, with the gift of a Kodak Brownie camera. The idea of one day turning my all-absorbing hobby into a career did not take root until my school's annual speech day, held at Ilford Town Hall, when I was fifteen.

The headmaster had just started his long-winded address when a fireman rushed onto the stage and announced that the High Street was ablaze and that the Town Hall would be evacuated (we were to be spared hours of chronic boredom).

As we trooped out in the gathering dusk, I slipped away to take a look at the fire. It was spectacular; the biggest blaze in Ilford since the war. As the inferno spread, I was transfixed by the sight of a man darting around, perilously close to the flames, taking photos: a press photographer from a local paper. Wow, what an exciting job, I thought. At that moment, I made up my mind.

The following day, I wrote to the editor of the *Ilford Recorder*, seeking advice. He wrote back, promising to have a chat with me when I had completed my studies. He was true to his word, and, at the tender age of sixteen, I joined the newspaper as a 'darkroom boy'.

I could not have wished for a better training ground. In the hurly-burly of a newsgathering operation, I mastered all aspects of photographic production, worked alongside seasoned professionals, adjusted to the pressure of deadlines and learnt to cope with irascible reporters.

The day came when I was entrusted with a Nikon and my role as a professional photographer began. The assignments were typical fare for local newspapers in those days: flower shows, civic functions, school fêtes, etc. Though not notably 'exciting', the jobs were always challenging – it is no mean feat to bring back a stunning photo from a cake show! The showbiz glamour and drama of foreign conflicts would come in later years.

As I had been brought up in neighbouring Barking before my family moved to Ilford, I was operating on home territory. I soon joined the newly launched *Newham Recorder* in East Ham, under the editorship of the legendary Tom Duncan, a Fleet Street veteran who brought the hard-edged standards of national journalism into a local arena. He was a tough taskmaster, demanding the highest standards of reporting and photographic coverage.

Duncan's crusading zeal was not always appreciated by the local authorities as, week after week, the newspaper highlighted the chronic problems confronting its readers.

A scandalous shortage of homes and the sub-standard conditions of much of the council accommodation headed the list of social ills, and the *Recorder*'s relentless campaign for improvements was given greater impetus by the shock effect of my photos.

Racial tension was another burning issue. The Afro-Caribbean families setting up home in the East End suffered widespread hostility and intimidation. Racist graffiti and threatening taunts were commonplace. Our newspaper was in the vanguard of the struggle for greater understanding and tolerance.

One typical day my assignment was to bring back a picture symbolising a more hopeful future – black and white children playing happily together in the street. I photographed two boys, the best of mates, who were taking it in turn to push each other in their go-cart. Reality for many immigrants was less rosy. The same evening I was sent to the home of a black family who, for many months, had been victims of a race-hate campaign. Along with threats of physical harm, their front door had been battered and daubed with racist graffiti. They lived in terror. Our coverage of their plight resulted in more police patrols in the neighbourhood.

Racism, poverty, families living in squalor, industrial unrest, crime, sport … there was no shortage of newsworthy topics, and there never seemed to be enough hours in the week to produce a journal that fully reflected life in our community.

When I switched to life as a freelancer, operating for both the national and local press, the entire East End became my canvas, from Aldgate to Leytonstone, from Hackney to the Isle of Dogs.

Despite the seemingly sameness of East London's terraced streets, the individual boroughs had their own character, at least in the minds of those living there – people in East Ham were likely to refer to residents of West Ham as members of a different tribe. There was still a shared pride in being a 'Cockney', especially among those of my parents' and grandparents' generation who had endured and survived the Blitz.

Few neighbourhoods had escaped the attentions of the Luftwaffe, and the process of regenerating bombsites and building new homes was painfully slow. Nobody could have foreseen that bomb-battered docklands and down-at-heel districts such as Limehouse, Hackney and Bow (fabled home to true Cockneys; those born within earshot of the church bells) would become the sought-after residential areas they are today.

While the Swinging Sixties' revolution in pop music, fashion and art made little impact on day-to-day life in my part of London, change was definitely in the air. I was aware that the social landscape was altering and that many of the vignettes of life around me would soon be gone. As an admirer of the early Victorian photographers and their archive from a vanished past, I spent my spare time seeking out scenes that captured the spirit of my own times, creating a record of 'ordinary' life in the Sixties.

A selection of those images appear in this book: cloth-capped men play cards in the all-male sanctuary of a pub's public bar; new tower blocks look out over a sea of rubble, where terraced streets were blitzed; an elderly man pushes a creaking bike on which a sign proudly proclaims, 'Complete Homes Purchased'; children use bombsites as their playgrounds; a market stallholder does brisk business selling cockles and whelks by the pint.

Some photos can be misleading, of course. The pictures I took in 1969 of people still living in 'temporary' wartime Nissan huts may convey a feeling of hardship, but, in fact, the families were extremely content in their corrugated-asbestos makeshifts and had no wish to be moved to a new tower block.

Sometimes a small detail lifts a photo. My close-up of an army disposal unit defusing a large German bomb is a case in point. It was a nerve-wracking job; all the more so when I noticed that the officer was smoking – and sprinkling fag ash and sparks on the still-active bomb (you can just see the cigarette in his hand).

In another image, the significant detail is a pram. A mini-skirted lollipop lady stands at a zebra crossing on a busy bus route. The charming touch is that the pram on the pavement is hers, and that she brought her baby with her every day, so combining day job with maternal duties.

Large parts of docklands, now London's showcase redevelopment, were still wasteland in the Sixties. As illustrated in these pages, the area was a magnet for hundreds of gipsy caravans. This community of nomads provoked the wrath of nearby residents, fuelling confrontations with the police as well as regular headlines in the local press. Disused buildings near the Royal Albert Docks were home to scores of meth drinkers, whose bleak lives I also chronicled.

East London was not without its sprinkling of stardust: the Rolling Stones played at the local Odeon, while Cliff Richard, Eartha Kitt, Frankie Vaughan and Adam Faith sang for their supper in recently opened nightspots. One afternoon I dropped in on former East Ham boy David Bailey, who had become the world's top fashion photographer, and persuaded him to pose in front of *my* camera with girlfriend Penelope Tree. (Me, envious? Nonsense.)

Returning from an assignment in Africa in the early Seventies, I was offered a job on a new London daily; I spent the next thirty-five years as staff photographer on the *Sun*. It was a hugely enjoyable period for me, though working in Fleet Street could be stressful and frenetic: I would often wake in the morning not knowing which country, let alone which city, I would be in by the evening.

After my retirement in 2006, I had time to look back through the East End negatives I had stored in the loft. I was immediately struck by the slower pace of life they evoked. The milkman I photographed pushing his heavy handcart around the back streets of Stratford, for example, appears totally in tune with the placid tempo of his work.

I was surprised to note how many horse-drawn vehicles there were on the roads half a century ago, with Steptoe-like totters ringing bells or blowing trumpets, coalmen and greengrocers making their rounds, market traders using old nags to haul their goods. My mother loved seeing these working horses in our street and always made a point of giving them lumps of sugar.

The rhythms of daily life have quickened dramatically since the Sixties, and many of the locations in which I worked have been face-lifted beyond recognition. Here is a glimpse of my East End – the way it was.

Steve Lewis, 2014

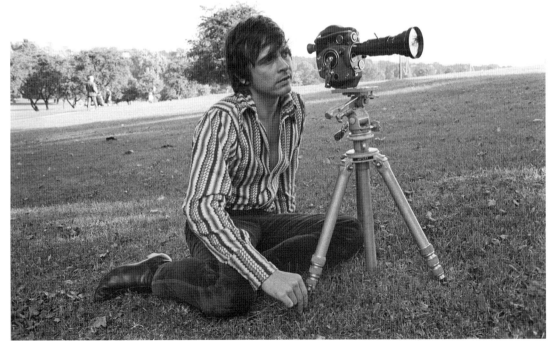

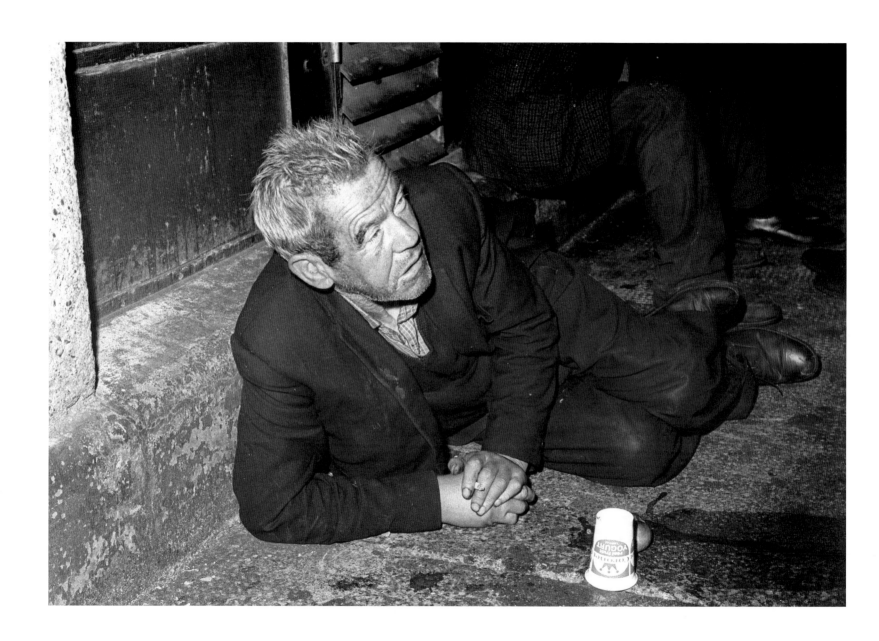

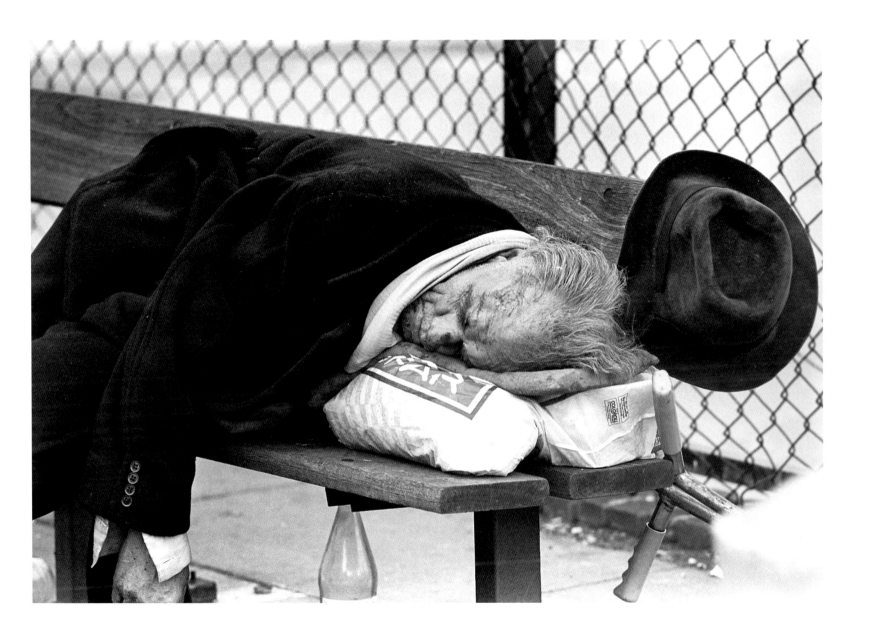

76

5 /-